Food Groups

Vegetables

Lola Schaefer

Heinemann LIBRARY

www.heinemann.co.uk/library
Visit our website to find out more information about Heinemann Library books.

To order:
☎ Phone 44 (0) 1865 888066
📄 Send a fax to 44 (0) 1865 314091
💻 Visit the Heinemann Bookshop at www.heinemann.co.uk/library to browse our catalogue and order online.

First published in Great Britain by Heinemann Library, Halley Court, Jordan Hill, Oxford OX2 8EJ, part of Pearson Education. Heinemann is a registered trademark of Pearson Education Ltd.

Editorial: Diyan Leake and Kristen Truhlar
Design: Joanna Hinton-Malivoire
Picture research: Melissa Allison
Artwork: Big Top
Production: Duncan Gilbert
Originated by Modern Age
Printed and bound in China by South China Printing Co. Ltd

ISBN 978 0 431 01518 7 (hardback)
12 11 10 09 08
10 9 8 7 6 5 4 3 2 1

ISBN 978 0 431 01525 5 (paperback)
12 11 10 09 08
10 9 8 7 6 5 4 3 2 1

British Library Cataloguing in Publication Data
Schaefer, Lola M., 1950-
 Vegetables. - (Food groups)
 1. Vegetables - Juvenile literature 2. Vegetables in human nutrition - Juvenile literature 3. Cookery (Vegetables) - Juvenile literature
 I. Title
 641.3'5

Acknowledgements
The publishers would like to thank the following for permission to reproduce photographs: © Corbis p. **20** (Royalty Free); © Getty Images pp. **14** (Photographers' Choice), **15** (Photodisc), **18** (StockFood Creative); © Harcourt Education Ltd pp. **4** (Tudor Photography), **10** (Tudor Photography), **13** (Tudor Photography), **16** (Tudor Photography), **19** (Tudor Photography), **21** (Tudor Photography), **22** (Tudor Photography), **23** (Tudor Photography), **24** (Tudor Photography), **26** (Tudor Photography), **27** (David Rigg); © istockphoto p. **11** (Andrew Cribb); © Photolibrary pp. **6** (Anthony Blake), **8** (Anthony Blake), **9** (Anthony Blake), **25** (Foodpix), **28** (Photononstop), **29** (Bill Bachman Photography); © Punchstock pp. **7** (Uppercut RF), **12** (Brand X).

Cover photograph reproduced with permission © Photolibrary.com (Anthony Blake).

Every effort has been made to contact copyright holders of any material reproduced in this book. Any omissions will be rectified in subsequent printings if notice is given to the publishers.

Disclaimer
All the Internet addresses (URLs) given in this book were valid at the time of going to press. However, due to the dynamic nature of the Internet, some addresses may have changed, or sites may have changed or ceased to exist since publication. While the author and publishers regret any inconvenience this may cause readers, no responsibility for any such changes can be accepted by either the author or publishers.

Contents

Some words are shown in bold, **like this**. You can find out what they mean by looking in the glossary.

What are vegetables?

Vegetables are parts of a plant eaten by people as food. Vegetables can be leaves, stems, or roots. Other vegetables are the flowers or the non-sweet fruit of the plant, such as peppers.

root vegetable

fruit vegetable

leaf vegetable

stem vegetable

flower vegetable

Each colour on this plate is for one of the five food groups.

Vegetables are one of the **food groups**. You need to eat vegetables every day as part of a good **diet**. Fresh vegetables help your body fight **diseases** and stay healthy.

Where vegetables come from

Vegetables grow on plants. Some people grow vegetables in their gardens. They plant seeds and wait for the plants to grow. They pick **ripe** vegetables and eat them.

Watching vegetables grow in your garden can be fun. Eating them is good, too.

When vegetables are ripe, they are picked and taken to shops to sell.

Vegetables are also grown in fields. Farmers drive large machines that plant vegetable seeds in rows. Some vegetables are grown in big greenhouses. These vegetables grow well in warm temperatures.

How vegetables are eaten

Many people eat fresh, **raw** vegetables. They eat them in salads, with dip, or just washed and cut up. Fresh, raw vegetables have the most **nutrients**. This means they have the **vitamins** and **minerals** that your body needs to stay healthy.

You can eat your favourite fresh vegetables with a tasty dip.

Steamed green vegetables are a healthy food at any meal.

Steaming vegetables is another healthy way to eat them. Some people bake, grill, or boil vegetables. Other people cook vegetables with different foods.

What vegetables look like

Vegetables grow in many shapes, colours, and sizes. Some vegetables are dark green, some are orange, others are light green, white, yellow, or red. Some vegetables are round and wide, others are long and thin.

Pumpkin and squash have a lot of **vitamins** C and E.

Fresh vegetables can look different than cooked vegetables. A pumpkin out of the field is big, round, and orange. Cooked pumpkin is still orange, but it is soft and has no shape.

How vegetables taste

Most vegetables have a **mild** taste. Radishes and a few other root vegetables can be **tangy**. If you eat **raw** vegetables, the taste will be stronger than if you eat them cooked.

These vegetables have stronger tastes when they are raw than when they are cooked.

Potatoes can be cooked in many different ways. When they are cooked, they become soft.

Most fresh vegetables like cucumber and celery are crisp. When vegetables are cooked, they become softer. Some people like to add **seasonings** to their vegetables.

Why vegetables are healthy

Vegetables are healthy because they are full of **nutrients**. They have **fibre, vitamins, minerals,** and good **carbohydrates**. Try and eat some **raw** vegetables every day.

Every raw vegetable is full of vitamins and minerals.

Eating vegetables helps keep the body strong and healthy so you can climb and play.

The nutrients in vegetables work together. They fight **diseases** and keep the body strong. They also heal **wounds** and keep eyes and skin healthy.

15

How many vegetables do you need?

Most children 5–10 years old need 1½–2 servings of vegetables a day. A handful of **raw** vegetables could be a serving. Two large spoonfuls of leafy vegetables like spinach or lettuce also make a serving.

Green, leafy vegetables are very good for you. They help protect against some **diseases**.

Each vegetable is full of nutrients for your body.

Try to eat many different kinds of vegetables. You should try to eat vegetables with a lot of different colours. Eating a mixture will give you the most **nutrients**.

Vegetables to eat for breakfast

Some people eat grilled tomatoes and mushrooms for breakfast. They might serve these vegetables with eggs. Some people eat potatoes for breakfast.

This healthy breakfast has vegetables and **protein**.

Juices can be made and stored in the refrigerator for a quick breakfast.

Drinking vegetable juice is a great way to start the day. Chilled tomato juice really fills you up. Vegetable juices can be made at home in a blender.

Vegetables to eat for lunch

Many people like to eat salads for lunch. You can make a mixed salad with lettuce and vegetables. You can make coleslaw with cabbage and carrots.

Salads are filled with **nutrients** so they are very good for your body.

Rainbow salad

Please ask an adult to help you.

- Mix all the vegetables together in a bowl.
- Add the rice vinegar and the brown rice syrup.
- Season with salt and pepper.
- Mix well and refrigerate for at least 30 minutes.
- Serve and enjoy.

You will need:
- 125 millilitres of rice vinegar
- 2 tablespoons honey
- 1 sliced cucumber
- 4 chopped tomatoes
- 1 chopped red onion
- salt and pepper to taste

This salad will serve you and a few friends.

Vegetables to eat for dinner

A bowl of hot vegetable soup is a good way to fill up at dinnertime. It is also a healthy meal. It tastes good with a whole grain bread roll.

Many different vegetables can go into a vegetable soup.

Vegetable soup

Please ask an adult to help you.

- Heat the butter and olive oil in a pan.
- Cook the onion, carrots, and red pepper for 3–4 minutes.
- Add the beans and mushrooms. Cook for another 2 minutes.
- Add the stock, water, potatoes, and a little salt and pepper.
- Bring to a boil, reduce the heat, and cover.
- Cook for 15–20 minutes, until the vegetables are soft.
- Serve and enjoy.

You will need:
- 1 tablespoon (tbsp) of butter
- 1 tbsp of olive oil
- 1 chopped onion
- 2 sliced carrots
- 1 chopped red pepper
- 1 handful of green beans
- 8 sliced mushrooms
- 2 large chopped potatoes
- 720 millilitres vegetable stock
- 360 millilitres water
- salt and pepper

Vegetables to eat for snacks

Vegetables are healthy snacks. Cherry tomatoes can be eaten whole. Carrots, celery, and peppers can be cut into small pieces and eaten fresh. Radishes are a one-bite snack.

Vegetables can go anywhere you go.

Tomato salsa

Please ask an adult to help you.

- Mix all of the ingredients together in a bowl.
- Cover and leave in the refrigerator for 2 hours.
- Serve and enjoy.

You will need:
- 6 chopped tomatoes
- 1 chopped red onion
- 1 large handful chopped coriander
- 1 chopped jalapeño pepper
- salt and pepper

Tortilla chips dipped in tomato salsa is a good snack to share with friends.

Keeping vegetables fresh

Many vegetables can be kept fresh by storing them in a cool, dark place. Potatoes and onions can be kept in a cool cabinet.

Store vegetables out of the light. They keep better in the dark.

The healthiest vegetables are firm and bright.

Leaf vegetables, like lettuce, need to be stored in the refrigerator. Peppers, carrots, and celery also need to be kept in the refrigerator. The cool air in the refrigerator helps keep the vegetables fresh.

Do vegetables alone keep you healthy?

Vegetables are good for your body. But you need to drink water and eat many other foods to stay healthy. Try and eat foods from each **food group** every day.

Drinking three or four big glasses of water each day helps keep your body working well.

Swimming uses many muscles and is very good for your body.

As well as eating healthy foods, your body needs regular **exercise**. You should try to get a little each day. You also need to get plenty of sleep each night. Sleep helps you stay strong and well.

Glossary

carbohydrate   part of food that gives a person energy

diet   what a person usually eats and drinks

disease   illness that keeps a person from normal day-to-day activities

exercise   physical activity that helps keep a body healthy and fit

fibre   rough part of food that is not digested. Fibre helps carry food through your body.

food group   foods that have the same kind of nutrients. There are five main food groups, plus oils.

mild   not sharp or strong in taste or odour

mineral   nutrient needed to make the body work correctly

nutrient   substance (such as a vitamin, mineral, or protein) that you need to stay healthy and grow

protein   nutrient in food that gives the body energy and helps it grow

raw   food that has not been cooked

ripe   fully grown and ready to pick or eat

seasoning   ingredient used to flavour food. Salt and pepper are seasonings.

steam   cook by putting food in a pan with hot water and mist

tangy   having a sharp or unusual flavour

vitamin   nutrient in food that the body needs to stay healthy and help the body work correctly

wound   injury in which the skin is torn, broken, or cut

Find out more

Books to read

Go Facts: Healthy Eating, Paul McEvoy (A & C Black, 2005)

Look After Yourself: Eat Healthy Food!, Angela Royston (Heinemann Library, 2004)

What's on Your Plate? Breakfast, Ted and Lola Schaefer (Raintree, 2006)

Websites to visit

www.5aday.nhs.uk
Click on "Fun & Games" and then "Did You Know?" to find out amazing vegetable facts.

www.childrenfirst.nhs.uk/kids/health/eat_smart/food_science/index.html
Click on the vegetables on the tray to find out more about why these are good for you and how many you need to eat each day.

www.nutrition.org.uk
Click on "Cook Club" for some great recipe ideas.

Index